The Book of *LIFE*

The Book of *LIFE*

poems

Joseph Campana

T|P

Tupelo Press
North Adams, Massachusetts

Library of Congress Cataloging-in-Publication Data available upon request.
ISBN: 978-946482-20-4

Cover and text designed and composed in Adobe Caslon Pro by Bill Kuch. Cover art: Robert Rauschenberg (American, 1925–2008). "Retroactive I," 1964. Oil and silkscreen ink on canvas, 84 x 60 in. (213.4 x 152.4 cm). Wadsworth Atheneum Museum of Art, Hartford, Connecticut. Gift of Susan Morse Hilles, 1964.30. Photograph: Allen Phillips/Wadsworth Atheneum. Used with permission.

First edition: March 2019.

Tupelo Press
P.O. Box 1767, North Adams, Massachusetts 01247
(413) 664–9611 / editor@tupelopress.org / www.tupelopress.org

Tupelo Press is an award-winning independent literary press that publishes fine fiction, nonfiction, and poetry in books that are a joy to hold as well as read. Tupelo Press is a registered 501(c)(3) nonprofit organization, and we rely on public support to carry out our mission of publishing extraordinary work that may be outside the realm of the large commercial publishers. Financial donations are welcome and are tax deductible.

Published with support of the City of Houston
through Houston Art Alliance

for my mother, Mary Campana,
daughter of Bernice

Contents

Envoi

Imagine your life is a movie. You
         are not so beautiful, would
not be cast in the movie that is your
         life, but the light might transfigure
even you, so you focus instead on
         the box. Not so special
sitting there, dullness of brown
         reinforced at the corners,
gestures of care expressed in strictures
         of tape. Gifts from your mother
(here, take them) but no doubt sealed
         by your father's hands, eager
for something to do. The movie would
         begin with the box, how it
beckoned, suspiciously still on the hand-
         wrought planks, perhaps some
decorative rug lazing beneath as trees
         cast an eerie green light
throughout the house. First the box,
         then the voice. "In the middle
of my life, there was a box." Maybe
         a voice-over about how thoroughly,
most days, the world refuses to
         acknowledge what you desire.
Take the box. Take what is given to you.
         Your life isn't a movie. No one
waits in line for you. But there
         was a box. There were floors,
no rugs at all. There were remnants
         of an age past. How much less lasting
they are, those near to us in time. You were
         waiting for a new life to seize you
but all you had was this box,

the painted legacy of *LIFE* magazines, sweet
and pungent whiff as paper crumbles
        to dust your fingers. You almost
think you can see the ink disaggregating
        before your eyes. It is, like most
things, too slow to be seen. "We're getting
        rid of them all." That was all she
said, urgency of another forgetting,
        no room for the past, except
that voice, first voice, voice singing
        words to me when I knew
I was you. When I knew not words but
        song alone and unending. That was
what lured me: the song of the world
        disappearing before me as I will too.
I write so I might disappear. So yes,
        I took it. I tried to seize
what was never mine just as in 1936
        Henry Luce seized *TIME* and *LIFE*.
He could see in his mind at night
        images that made *the American century,*
enormities glimmering in the faces and sketches.
        What was it I desired, there, in the middle
of a life scarcely lived, a life buried in pages?
        Not in 1936 nor at 36 could I tell you.
And the years kept passing, all the pages
        passing so swift and delicate they might tear
as I touched them. Didn't I want them to tear?
        Didn't I want history to rip itself open
and take me in? Green light on the brown box
        and the box that moved as I moved
and waited for me as the world would and
        when I could not, when stuck, somewhere,
unable to travel downstream in the lush
        wake of time to wherever history
would take me. I didn't have a story, which is

not to say I didn't have a past, but
no one transfigured me in black and white.
        If I write to tell you, dear reader, I
was changed, you'd have to care what I
        had been and what I was coming
to be as another American century passed
        and left me behind. Green on brown,
the dense leaves around the house protecting
        me from death and convergence,
from life in time. Imagine you could say, *This*
        is the middle of my life. Here it happened.
Whatever it was. But it did not happen in the middle.
        Don't you remember? Late, once, in
the ancient dark of night, you looked up
        and some celestial woman gazed down.
Mother of infinite stars, here I am. This is
        my story now. Every word was your gift,
and every word, Mother, I return to you.
        Now, I am ready to begin.

First Issue

November 23, 1936

Scream of beginnings: what was once sequestered now haul into light. There was a camera for you: there is always a camera ready. All will be seen, the child now dangling from the hands of the miracle man. Once you were poised between lives, an un-breathing thing. Now plunge into this one, this life. Enter, now, *LIFE*. All enter like patient passengers lining up for transport, tickets in hand, a team of nurses in the background to usher them through to destinations not yet final. Oh nurse of life, complete in your un-attachment to me or to anyone or to basins of porcelain, blood in water, sheets disarrayed but perhaps staged for the camera. How much trouble can one life make, passing through what it will pass out of at some as yet undetermined date? Come, child, enter the field of vision with a red-faced cry. You already have secrets to tell the glass. Somewhere in the background your mother has disappeared behind the doctor and nurses. Look: imagine the camera is your mother. Cry to her, child, cry of beginnings. The engine of your life waits. The flywheel is already spinning up.

Sing of the disappearances: "New Deal." No longer merely an idea in 1936. Now it's a shack town of bartenders, sellers of snakeoil, mechanics, and hairdressers to the wives of the men who will raise stone and steel to stare down the river. Every-one can be different in New Deal, Montana, in Square Deal, Montana, in Delano Heights. The great man made a promise. The great man wants you to be happy. He puts the water to work for you as he puts you to work for America. Men perch on the spokes of a great wheel destined to be driven into earth.

Oh conduit, oh cloud-capped crenellations! One minute floods of men. The next, floods of water. Who will rise higher? I can't find you anywhere: you are a map without a place. The great man has sunk deep beneath enclosing waters and will not return. The great wheel turns its quickened symmetry to current. Some will rise with it. Some can only fall.

There is a city in the sky so far from Montana that birds, when they wheel through those clouds, brush the hands of Christ. In this city, the rivers are rain wept of envy for the beauty of the shore. What they would do for such beauty was only the first mistake. In the dream of 1936, there is a city that cares little for industry. Imagine that, the wide-open arms of the one who would save you from yourself. In what plenty you might live: rubber and sugar only a taste of the vast crops of a garden of Eden. Years ago, the city went by another name and over its shores rose a man sprouting arrows. Years ago, like us, they were willing to work to death to submit the river. Progress, we named you Fort Peck, but still you will not speak. Tell us, will we lose ourselves in water?

Time in its wisdom, time in its disclosing of marvels at last recorded on August 6, 1934, when the great man marked the stone with his words and counted the *countless tributaries that run into it and countless other tributaries that run into those tributaries.* Time streaming. Time flooding. Every moment more distant from some never-measured point. Time receding, the dam decaying before your eyes. If you could only see it, you would note the infinitely patient progress of time. Fort Peck, it was 1943 when you finally harnessed the river. Some small dominion was yours. Oh engines of ruthless time, forces of earth and river which will not willingly yield up these mysteries. Speak now, river. Say, "Here it begins!" even as time, undisclosed, obscures its own beginning. Oh engine, water, terrifying in your infinite plasticity, imagine it all begins with you.

You imagine you can remember how dark it was and how, surrounded by water, the first longing was the yearning to escape into the ruthless streams of time. What wouldn't you do to start the wheels and pulleys, time now harnessed, now yours, now to hand. It's as if you could reach into water and cup time in your palm. Look there, your own face stares back up from the pool of water that is your hand in labor. The dam will rise, the dam will hold, the dam will wall back time. Death in his inky cloak will not come for us. He is not yet knocking at the gate.

In the beginning there was water. I can't remember the passage here, only what would not be held back. River water, heartwater: Missouri River nourished by mountains I've never seen. Water before the unities of time and place. So much I've never seen. Sometimes I imagine I could stand high atop the Fort Peck Dam and see everything that is this America: whatever it was in 1936, whatever it is now. Always more an idea than what it really is, a dam so big the population of Tennessee could stand on its surface. That's not to speak of the dredging, the unobliging inner territories of a continent, the building of a shipyard, the painful weight of clay and shale, ships sailing an America pristine and unpeopled. There is only water, the memory of water, and a riot of power streaming to all tributaries.

Someone's always talking about it. The hope of pointing to it, of a finger curling around like it might caress a trigger. Not fire but water: first mover, all-engulfing. This was where the trouble was bound to arise. No need to breathe: you're surrounded. In the book of the life you imagine you lead, somewhere must be written, "Here it begins." When did the terror come, or was that always the way beginning was supposed to feel? Water the concealer, water the deliverer, water the deep. Before the rivers rose up at a command, before the unities of time and place were assembled, someone stood terrified before the vast wash of the new wondering, *What's starting up? Who is about to begin?*

Late in '38

October 17, 1938

1.

Late in '38, I asked if,
if nothing else, a few
small things would be
better off for our having
been here. I thought she
would smile. Always
she was quick to smile.

2.

You begin with
the cover. No one
smiles. Were you
to write it all down
you would say with
infinite compassion
she saw the world
burn before her.

3.

Wake up, she said,
wake up, it's 1938.
The world flickers.
The world is what
is waiting to be lit.

4.

Of the thirty-eight
ways I'd make
her immortal, I
choose this: not
with a kiss but
with what a face
makes when it
cannot smile.

5.

Imagine hidden
somewhere in
the magazine
there is a gesture of
infinite compassion.
Believe you will
find it. Flip so
quickly the pages
rip at your touch.

6.

Not so funny, now. Each
photo a story, each story
an instant's decision: who
to love or save or bury in
history's patent obscurity.

7.

Someday someone will find
the woman on page fifty-six.
It will seem as if she had
been smiling all this time.

8.

Such signs as these,
such sad, strange stage
plays in the large and
dismal theater of history
suggested, to *LIFE*,
the nearing end. For
once, the screaming
was real, but you were
not, just then, screaming.

9.

There is no woman
on page fifty-six.
There are only
images of faces
designed to enflame.

10.

That was your mistake.
All this time you thought
you could almost touch
the flowers on her collar,

that she would be
the one to love you
for who you really are.

11.

Once upon a time there
was a luminous blonde.
Once here, now gone.
No hint of smile to light
the world. *Luminous
blonde,* I said, *what
is the world?* She said,
*The world is the sad
mirror in which you
see your face alone.*

Praise for the Snow

April 17, 1944

Praise for the snow in Central Park, April

       buds frosted white and now somehow

more than they were. Praise for Kansas City,

       Missouri: heart of a nation at war, eye

and center of some final revelation composed

of hapless remainders, those subject to the gathering,

       archive of what might have but did not last.

Praise for the leather satchels laboriously

       stitched, the duffel bags haplessly slung,

suitcases with their stripes, stamped crates

       with their blazoned letters

       and the bags full, the bags full

of the emptiness of abandoned time. Praise

       for the reachers, for those who know to grasp.

Every recess can be searched, every clasp can be opened.

       What is left in a pocket

if not the feeling of someone else's

hand? Praise for pictures strewn on

a battlefield: girl with a gleaming trombone, girl

with a fresh-baked pie. No, really.

I saw her holding it out as a way of reaching

across the seas. I could almost smell

how tart the apples, how fecund the earth,

and how there lingered, on the surface of the image,

flecks of a distant battlefield.

I don't know where all the bodies went.

I have a receipt for remittance and a claim on a parcel of

goods. Praise for the sharp-edged, coins layered with

dirt. The South Seas and their finest tender come

with words of wisdom in a faded pamphlet:

"Meet New Zealand." I'd really like that.

I'd like to meet them all in Central Park under April

boughs, the boughs unexpectedly jeweled. This is

Kansas City, Missouri, gateway to the West

and all its unwary fantasies realized in

the burial ground of the accumulations,

buttons in their infinite arrays,

letters and diaries urgent in repetition,

collections of the tiny practicalities,

the sewing kits assigned each boy,

whether his fingers were nimble

or not. I could never hold one

steady enough. I could never reach that far.

Praise the steady and the supple:

those who believe in repair. And praise

the many, the inadvertent, the left back

sorters of queasy treasures. Guardians

of the hundreds: buttons

without shirts, shirts without end, shoes

laid out on a desk with the care of angels.

Meanwhile the World

January 30, 1948

"The light has gone from our lives and there is
darkness everywhere."
                                        Jawaharlal Nehru

1.

Meanwhile, the world.
Everything turning.

2.

It was just what
I thought you'd do,
stand on your head
as capitols burned.
Somehow, all those
buildings remained
perfectly pristine:
Boise, Lincoln,
Bismarck, Lansing,
Cheyenne. As a child
you learned them all,
praying to places
you might never be:
away, away, away.

3.

I watched him even then—
man with his wheel
spinning the world.

4.

Imagine Schenectady,
not yet city of my
father, 1948: the ice
carnival, a stunt skater
trips on a loop of
flame, ignites his
burning face. *Fire
or ice,* the poet said,
both suffice.

5.

By the river, stairs
to the water. Even
the river burns.

6.

So the great one died.
Then it was over,
meaning it would
never be over. At
the St. Paul Winter
Carnival, men and
cars made a great
circumference in the
ice of White Bear
Lake. If you could see
it as I do, from high
above, it would
beggar description.
By fire, by ice, turn,
great wheel.

7.

Meanwhile the world.
Everything burning.

8.

Tell me, I said,
what is the dark?
And you said,
Love, I am the dark.
I am the black
word, the page
at the end
of all that is.

9.

"So much waste,"
the poet said as he
shaped, "so many
things that don't
strike fire."

10.

In the middle
of the century,
bats trained
to set cities
ablaze, each
one-ounce bomb
burning for

eight minutes
with a twenty-
two-inch flame.

11.

A million faces
crowd about
one solitary fire.
You are one
of this multitude.
You hear flame
crack open the world:
By this heat, warm
your tender bodies.
By this light,
see your face.

12.

Each spoke of
the wheel some
indifferent image,
each circle of
thread a star.

13.

I would say to the sky
I would say to the bomb
You won't come to harm, I
would say to the sky,
Your open eyes

Your face a balm
I would speak to the sky, I
would speak to the bomb.

14.

Mohandas Karamchand
Gandhi consigned
to flame:
January 31, 1948.

15.

It was as if I carried
them myself, each page
freighted with twelve
hundred pounds of
sandalwood, three
hundred twenty pounds
of ghee, one hundred
sixty pounds of incense,
thirty pounds of swift
camphor, an undetermined
number of flowers and
the weight of fourteen
hours. This is what it
takes to burn a body,
each page a wick and
the wick was shame.

16.

One man runs a
circle. Run, man,

run. A new world
waits at the end of
the circle that
never ends.

17.

"I do not want to live,"
the great one said,
"in darkness and madness."

18.

Ice made a world
around you. Lake
Placid, Olympic
rings circle
a century never
to come again:
1932, 1980.
Everyone
gathered, circles
of eyes around
a television. Six
years old I saw
steel slash ice,
bodies skidding
terribly against
one another,
exhilarating
grace followed
by impact, as
when a car spins

off a road, how
slow until it is
over, the body
stilled for just
one moment,
all forms of ice
connected here,
Lake Placid,
beautiful thought:
the wheel will
hold back rage,
these bodies now
one, the linked arms,
the singular kiss.

19.

Meanwhile the world:
everything burning,
everything turning,
wheel that will not end.

Grip the Rope

March 6, 1950

Teeth clenched the boy grips the rope, his hair shorn.

The rope he grips grips back, the rope wrapping around
the body of the beast.

The body bucks of its own accord, its mind being free:
the only pain is the clenched jaw, the tight grip, the rope
held and the hair shorn short, tight.

The boy tangled in the rope is not my father grimacing,
born cold: the coal gone, the mines closed, the sea
closing over bars of silver.

Hands close over bars of silver to drag them into the light.

The man lit by the glow of silver is not my father lit
by the shape of a new Motorola: 1950.

My father alone in the black and white box, his hand grips
the paddle of a fur trader's boat trading up and down
the Mississippi, 1832, his hand clenched grips the gun
as the harpoon pierces the delicate flesh of the catch.

The claws of the lion clutch the ground like the soles of
good shoes: Samson the good grimaces as his blind eyes
grasp an unseen world. The temple crashes down.

It is better not to see the boy crashing down, the ice hard,
Holland cold, the skates sharp to touch.

My father razors across the ice, time sharp in the light
of a castle burning. Is something born there, burning,
escaping into the night?

Something born of the cold night. March frozen open
anyway. Father, small one: unclench your hands.

Father, small one: be born here. Oh, to be born.

A Shirt Loves a Body

December 7, 1953

A shirt loves a body the way
a bracelet kisses a wrist, kisses
the tender flesh stretched over
tendon and vein: a whole world
thrumming just below. Fingers
love motion the way the flesh
loves the deep electrical twitch
of the body involuntary, satisfied
with itself and one at last with
a music that loves to fill a room
the way a piano loves Liberace
and Victor Borge. Chrysler loves
soldiers the way a mother loves
a child, which strangely enough
is not unlike the way Santa Claus
loves toasters, deep fryers, coffee
makers, and electric razors all for
the gift of their shiny utility. Oh,
Pyrex, oh Playtex: contain contain
contain the ease of abundance,
which loves to billow and fill
a house the very way a chimney
loves smoke, the way all conduits
of transport love vicious motion:
the silky burn of a Pall Mall
searing like a car yearns for
one great and final acceleration
that can release only into starry
conflagrations under a watchful
desert sun. The desert loves sun
almost as much as it loves secrets

just as a fugitive loves Texas
and all solitary expanses of
passage unimpeded by custom.
Lovers love love and even more
they love to play dead. Imagine
the world whole and uninterrupted
by a desire for witness, the world
indifferent to all things pertaining,
the lovers now like statues buried
in the desert sand or hidden in
a dark cave that aches for collapse.
Chanel No. 5 loves Chanel No. 5
and wears nothing else to bed.
Naked, at last, it is finally itself
alone, vapors free in the night
air and practically fire now,
loving itself purely, the way
everyone loves useless gifts,
along with all other forms of
generosity indifferent to duty.
Imagine that: someone loved
you enough not to care, the way
a train, uninterested in terminus,
loves the interstitial hum of
tracks. Certain of their own end,
elephants love trains that speed
from darkened tents. Pull back
the flaps if you dare: all those
circles filled with the round "O"s
of faces tormented by wonder,
stretched by their own credulity
until the body becomes a letter
that would tell you precisely how
a body loves if only you could
read it. Slack-jawed, wide-eyed,
open-mouthed: the body one great

aperture. That's how it loves,
in the manner of the sky that
loves the foolish conveyances
of tiny creatures so ambitious
for transport, and the sky loves
them all, nearly as much as
the shirt, simple covering,
loves the press of flesh beneath
diffident folds, loves the way
fabric caresses a body just as
the eye strokes the camera,
a shoulder cradles a phone,
and the phone tenderly carries
voices gathering a line from
so far away. How could they sound
so close? And it is just this close,
the way a mother cradles the child
she sees she can no longer hold.

Fall of a Star

April 20, 1959

In the corner, in the living room,
someone waits. Outside, at last,
Mayflower Transit approaches.
Readiness is all: furnishings
to make a woman what she is
in the pictures. In the clear and
obvious wrap of their packages,
cigarillos await the moment of
ignition. In Bad Creek, Kentucky,
near Greasy Fork, three children
watch the midwife, waiting to hear
the cry of new life. In the sink,
immersed, the Coffeematic waits
for water to douse its spark. It
never happens. The coffee is
perfect every time. Seven young
men wait for the crushing force
of flight, their fingers all pointing
to the same heavens. Just then,
no stars were visible. One girl
waits for a prince to make her his
princess. Pearls ring her neck.
Diamonds catch in her teeth.
The stones wait to break what
they touch. Billy Wilder waits
for smoke to clear to reveal his
star. In the jail yard, toughs wait
for a blonde to bring them a loaf
of bread baked around a hacksaw.
The blonde never comes. The men
wait for someone else to stumble:

someone's always about to fall.
Perched on a gilded vanity, Maria
Callas waits for redemption. Her
heart is pure in the manner of those
unmerciful angels who stand, who
wait. Her voice rises above the
tedious swell of rumor's many
tongues. Everyone waited for a
world that would respond to touch.
Each hand extended, none accepted.
The vast wastes of the frozen
north waited for settlers to arrive.
Detroit was far. The new land
anticipated its clearing. It was
indifferent to faces blinking hope.
The face on the cover waited
for vindication. In her teeth
sparkled diamonds of inestimable
recalcitrance. In her body lived
some form of hope. It was resting
there in her heart. Darkness was
the waiting that swallowed hope,
dark like a black stone waiting
to be crushed into a jewel.

Fall of a Star

November 9, 1959

Teeth clenched, the star arched
in a manner suggesting the shape
of other women: Lillian Russell,
Theda Bara, Jean Harlow, Marlene
Dietrich. *Hope, hope, hope,* she
wrote in 1956 of another marriage
destined to end, but in 1959 she
leapt into the air, only one of
a number of luminaries: Brigitte
Bardot, Audrey Hepburn, Sophia
Loren, all, as the photographer
put it, *child-women, who have
been raised to the level of goddesses
by insecure men.* You can tell
everything by the way a body
surrenders the ground. Watch
Richard Nixon rise as Adlai
Stevenson falls. See J. Robert
Oppenheimer launch his slender
body upward, one finger nearly
touching the sky. *I was just
reaching,* he said, just reaching
into a sky lit by the radiance
of innumerable suns, the whole
world full of infinite possibility
in the form of death. Death,
destroyer of worlds, comes in his
dark suit for the woman in black,
Marilyn Monroe, leaping above
a barren shore, her legs pinned
behind her body. In 1962 no hope

remained, no body cast off
the weight of earthly obligation.
What won't appear in the magazines
appears in the morgue, surly snapshot
of a bitter end: the hair cascading
down, the skin and flesh sinking
down like the dusky brim of
a mushroom cloud, the world
so hot, so full of motes of starry
dust hidden in the dark privacies
of plain sight that everything rises
just long enough to fall back down.

Drops from the rafters.
By the door, my mother.

I was too small to see
how it hung there as blood

soaked the earth below.
Dampness of rotting wood,

of stale hay and draining pig,
sting and itch of fields

long dead through which,
as a child, she did not run.

Mother, carve me
a piece of what is left

swaying in the past
when you take me home.

Chanel No. 5

I don't know when she first tasted
the scent of this number, dragged
from a port where my father was stationed:
seeing the sights, fleeing his family,
but mainly thinking of her, writing
letters I think they never kept.

Fifteen when they met, eighteen
when married: three between
without sight, without scent
of anything but paper and pen
and was it hope or regret pressed
onto woody flesh as redolent as
her home: shattered stalks, crops
growing smaller, sadder each year.

If I asked her why she loved it, how,
having rarely left that farm, she could
tell this scent from so many others, if
I asked why memory became liquid
then vapor, she might not understand
my desire to know how insubstantial
filaments could tie two such bodies
together over oceans of tremulous time.

Now in the airport: shelves of the glittering,
bottles of essence of every number.
I won't buy any for all the women
I'll never marry, for all the men I'll love,
for all the children I may never raise,
or even for the mother who taught me
nearly everything. Because the one bottle

I do want doesn't contain the scent of how
to be a woman, but how, like my mother,
to love what you can't understand.

Corn silk
and the squawk
        of husking ears,
boiling water. Cake
        glistening the counter,
lawnmower ripping
        to life. The door
too swollen
        with age to shut.

November

Mother's cranberry, canned, slides a lump

from a tinny hovel. We are marked by our

encasements. Gelatinous love slicing parts

for all: delectation: my heart squishes a plate.

Texture's rot anyway, food a toy for your

winding down, your spinning and bagging

and wrapping and sleep. Thank you, I must

thank you. Cans ratchet open, line on line:

oh my nutritive empery. Someone draws you

from a darkening shelf. Someone slapped a

wing from the sky. Dress, dress, dress you

in flesh. Wear your belly to the table. Eat, eat,

eat your fillings. Someone's baked a pie from

canned blackbirds, someone pries open your song.

Night, mother
of day, of the bright air:
        you think of her
as a certain picture,
        a certain smile,
her hair spilling
        down its length, its
darkening riches
        cover you.
Who can tell the story
        of what comes
before night? This
        is what history is:
someone's falling,
        someone's leaving.

Wrinkle

your lungs fill a hospital, your $50 scream

someone lifts the squalling body: force of the sinister hand

your sex, your uncertainty a lit cigar

your sister tells you the story

someone's father's father, your girlish disappointments

wheel the thing from one machine to the next

the green he takes in the other hand, it is right

she would drink your blood if she weren't drinking her own

you flesh, you stem, you your mother's redolence

which is the hand that holds, that strikes, that will dispense?

smoke billowing over a crib

he has arrived, he's arrived—you can start your dying now

you were the brother of envy, the sister of doubt

that song was never yours, that song was never offered you

the men they smile they nod: where has your mother gone?

time will stretch the skin smooth as a fresh-pressed bill

from mouth to mouth, from hand to hand—

take it: green stalk of longing

what are you worth anyway?

In the picture your grandfather
holds you: what to do with this flesh?

You still glowing, wet with birth
and the camera your father's hand.

And it is your mother, maybe,
guiding his arm to her father.

Here, you can read her mind.
You feel her tighten like a frame.

Practice

It's three a.m. when I hear once more the repetition of scales I ought to know, did know, when, years ago and in an alien register, I squeezed the same ladders of tone from a clarinet now gathering moss in a closet far from here. I stopped playing when I stopped feeling extraordinary.

Nothing saves you in the night. No great cloak of quiet stills the pulsing organs of sense and the mind, too, is an organ of sense so hungry to be put to sleep that it cries for a dark forest of sound to muffle the blasts of light and fortune that sting and deliver to day the singular voice that knows only to sing and to leave behind its signature errors.

Each time it's the same: absence of error, absence of inspiration, though I sense that familiar hesitation. Tumble of pitches, smoothness of ivory though how much less haunting than the woody grief I inflicted on my parents with a spring of latches: Concerto for Clarinet in A (Adagio).

Death is a little closer, and the stillest music twitches my fingers into the only song I know.

Each week Mozart was dying in my parents' living room, dying before doors my mother closed for shame. Each week for nearly a year we relished clever Wolfgang moribund Wolfgang debauched Wolfgang. My father, who I'd rarely seen wash a glass, served lemonade, whispered conviviality, like someone I'd never met.

Listen to you: bird crying high into the trees.

Mr. Scheer worked other marvels, such transformations, designing machines to refine from merest matter the perfect reed. All too well I understood his fascination but not half so well as my mother understood Mozart. Inasmuch as I played it, she loved it: loved wrong notes she never heard, loved cadenzas I'd never write, loved even the life I sealed in a box in the dark where that music was heard from afar, absent of implication.

I won't close the window tonight no matter how painful it is to feel in the tips, in the knuckles of my hands, notes I could never reach racing to where they begin and I end, in vicious contemplation, the end of music.

***

Punishment is the way it seems to be talent filling the room: the case clicking shut and the latches squeezing down.

***

Does it matter that I cannot actually feel when you take your hands from your lap and set them on the beast before you with its white bones and black teeth and the steely lengths of tone from which I might, if I were clever, divine either mood or placement of hands or a sense of the breathless fury that drove you up the steps and before the strict engine of song you pedal toward me?

***

Tonight I feel the infinite sadness of care as I forget to attend the things of this world: breaking the instrument into its constituents and swabbing its humid innards with a purple cloth incapable of concealing the way the body spends itself and heaves about to make song. The only song I knew I played in the shameless anticipation of transport.

You are your song, and soon you'll be over.

Do you remember when I started this poem? We were sure of nothing then but departure. Tonight I hear them again and feel in the bones of my hands, in fingers that would never learn to open the world, how those few simple tones came to be bound. There is that still quality in the air again, a man placing his hands on cold keys because that is all there is before him. In the kitchen, his mother hums the notes she taught him. Now I hear them too. Now I am ready to begin.

❖

Of course, you
barely know yourself:
always going to,
ever coming from.

❖

Myth

The road in the dream is not a road. The dream is a book. In the book, a child stands on a dark street. The street is quiet therefore the child isn't crying. He's waiting for a car. There are no lines painted on the street. The street is new and the houses, which are not houses, are also relatively new. If there were lines on the street the child would be standing with his feet carefully placed, seeking the center. The child, you may assume, is cold and therefore not symbolic. I think it must be October. There are no cars passing by. If this were a different story, the doors to the nearest houses would open: quadrilateral spaces of light intruding on solitude. The boy would be able to see his breath. In the house next door, bursts of televisual radiance in the flickering darkness. Overhead: wheeling of the starry bones. The child can't name them. There's simply no time for myth. If your mouth were square it could open and from it would issue light.

They were
medals and whispers,
        rough weather
we no longer feared,
        flashes in the sky.

Total Eclipse

The world is ending
and all I can think of
is that song, that useless
song the unpopular girls
loved. Eighth grade,
the talent show, and
everyone wants to sing:
all the unpopular girls
who dance their pain
across the stage, hiking
up sequined tops that
refuse their awkward
bodies. My friends in
Dorset say darkness
won't reach them,
they say they'll drive
to Cornwall, to Land's
End, to Wales to get
a sense of the end,
but all I think of is
that day in Montreal,
with you, on the bus.
I wasn't even holding
your hand when a man
scowled and brushed
away the filth we carried
from the streets. Here
we are again, but the city
has changed. No one
sees nothing passing over.

It was my grandfather at the door.
That he had been dead for years
didn't bother me: it was his tone of voice.

He said, *Being dead is like*
hunger without the will to eat.
You forget the pangs.

He looked tired. I forgave him
and did the dishes. He played solitaire.
We both waited for the dream to end.

Reference

Your skin is fire, the red leather

you cling to. Old man folds the paper

to his liking, over and again. He

crinkles. You shouldn't be here:

this is what it means to read.

Outside, a whole world you have

no right to. You don't want it.

A soft rain settles on the houses.

In one of them your father sleeps.

He wakes when you go to bed, ties

his shoes, drags a thermos of steam

into the night. You dream of books.

You never know what else to ask for.

Afternoons your mother opens and

closes them, bringing down the stamp

again and again, red, she numbers them,

gently. She's giving them away. Who

are you waiting for? The chair stares

with dozens of golden eyes; it will not speak.

Hands wither
diamonds, her hands
bury hearts.
I can still hear cards
clicking down
the hours: club on
diamond, spade
in heart: people will
land where
they ought to land.

First Job

All evening I hunted
the bird that wanted
a cage of glass,
here where cemetery
slides into creek, fronting
what was once the largest
indoor leather mill in the world.
There the skins gathered
for cleansing, coloring,
scraping, shipping off.

It closed three years after
a lone sparrow set up camp
behind the only desk
in the only full-serve
service station left in town
where, from four to seven
nightly one summer,
I blackened the pages
of books with my thumbs.

Whatever it sought there—
thumping its frightened body
against glass, into cabinets
or out to the bays
scrubbed raw with gasoline
where the broken waited
to be raised up, hosed off,
fastened together in hope
of coughing to life again—
whatever it sought was not
a dollar slipped through
a window cracked because

patronage was right
for the aging ladies of August
to provide from Chryslers
cool in the sun.

There was nothing to be found
in books or boxes of parts.
And the tools hanging from pegs
were as useless as my hands,
which could not patch together
those straggling conveyances
any more than I could
with a tattered broom
batter the bird to freedom
as I swung at fluttering terror
as I sought with useless devices
some fortune reposed
in corners of grease and dust.

❂

Rushing past
gates like the child
I never was: so many
places to go, so many
conclusions we'd never
reach: the terminal
stretching for miles,
the planes frozen
to the runways.

❂

AMC Hornet, 1974

Road is memory—wax in sun.
                  Ahead, summer steam.
           Behind, Hornet in a yard, nighttime, moonstruck.
Window broken—my sister's hand. Blood on glass
                sparkling, the glass scattering in wind.

Sleep came easy then, time dragged us
           into darkness with its voices
(the sun isn't angry, the moon isn't crying)
              even the night we rode out bundled
(pull your head out of sleep)
                  skating on a lake of cold
where the orange beast waited
          to whir to life: mother's first car.

We were drones in the family way:
          without sweet, without queen.
Flock of bristling, wings without knowledge of flight
          though my mother set out alone.
We waited weeks
          for the rental to return, for her father to die.

Buzz of engine, sea of streets. My mother and I
          and the Hornet that spluttered and died and I
was happy, marooned with her there. She cried
          and I knew she hated my father, his father,
for coming, for putting it right.

Moonstruck driveway, sleepless whine.
Voices pooling in moist air,
running up street lamps, sliding through glass, whispering:
sun gave you wings, you didn't want them.
Papa gave you wings but no sting.

Imagine the Moon

September 12, 1962

Imagine the moon. Imagine there is a place beyond change. Imagine time pooling there, condensed, becoming what it would be, smaller than should be possible. Imagine time gathering to a place the size of Texas. Relative to the starry heavens Texas would be little more than a bullet.

When I looked into darkness, I saw no escape. *Look again,* I said to myself, *look again and see.* But still I did not see.

I heard it first: one simple crack as the world broke. There was no squealing of tires on the film. You remember watching it over and over. Without sound there are only explosions of will in terrifying expanses of space ungoverned by the pull of solid bodies. How fast they move when they break, those solid bodies.

Later, you'll remember this night.

Blood suddenly. Blood suddenly and like itself. Blood suddenly like an explosion of stars inaudibly far away.

"William Bradford, speaking in 1630 of the founding of the Plymouth Bay Colony, said all great and honorable actions are accompanied with great difficulties, and both must be enterprised and overcome with answerable courage."

To whom should my courage, such as it is, be answerable?

The little dying ones set sail on what seemed to be a new sea. There was nowhere else to go for the unsleeping children of night. They would not let our eyes close long enough to dream. *That's why,* you said, *there are stars.* But why, I asked. *To count the dreams you could not have.*

we choose we choose we choose we choose the moon

Imagine the climb, from cell to sea, sea to seafarer charting waves with wind caught in the skins of animals, from child to sailor of stars. Knowing not what awaits is the point.

It will be done before the end. *And then?* Then it will end.

The great leap, the small step, the small window looking out over the facets of a creation indifferent and only just visible to the dying ones. All the indifferent staring up at the same pendant moon. Everything is there to be reached.

Sing, Apollo, of the magnificent desolation.

And the moon and the planets are there. And the sun is there, bright herald, and the infinite darkness is there as are all the tiny instances of land in vacuous seas, jagged masses to scratch and grasp at the glassy borders of sight. I said, *But what are they there for?* You said, *For the grasping.*

Remember, starry ones, night will always be night.

With no more than the skins of animals. With little more than a cart, a prick-sharp nail. With little more than the black-stained blood of a press, the letters pounding the world to a roundness exceeded only by the smoothness of a wheel. Wheel of space spinning a compass, flywheel spinning an engine. The sizzle of the wires and a sudden flicker of day. Once, in this unrelenting night, I saw the one who would wheel us heavenward, straight to the moon.

Say them: Saturn, Mariner, Voyager, Mercury, Gemini, Pioneer, Pathfinder, Viking, Ceres, Galileo, Genesis, Ulysses, Dawn, Magellan, Apollo, Apollo, Apollo, sing, Apollo: far-darter, light-born, slayer of darkness, protector of the fields in which the future speaks its golden truths.

Later you'll remember this night. Then, the night will pass.

Thirteen, dreaming of space in the magnificent desolation of my room. Kennedy long dead. A line about asking. A line about destiny. One line for choice. What could the words still mean? Each night I looked up in the hope some as yet unwatched celestial body would look down upon the dark, tarry earth to which I clung and then would name me.

A Face in the Mail

June 21, 1963

Another year flips, another
face arrives in the mail. Every
year a page, every word
another clue to the puzzle
of rage. Everyone was in
love with Shirley MacLaine
in *Irma la Douce,* even
the police. Then, again,
everyone is lovable in Paris,
even if nowhere else. My
first time there I was stupid
with light but not yet in love.
If to know love is to know
the intimacy of rage, then it's
true to say I understood neither
anger nor love. The city was
such a wonder it didn't matter.
What does matter to me, this
day, is whether or not it is fair
to say that, on June 11, 1963,
when Quang Duc set himself
aflame, anger lit the wick. Ten
days later LIFE called him "an
angry Buddhist," who, flanked
by other Buddhists, "before
their reverent eyes struck a match
and set himself on flame." Oddly
poetic for a magazine, it's true,
as were the images. I think there
weren't enough pixels in 1963
to convey what alarm onlookers

must have felt as they steeled
themselves to honor whatever
gesture they imagined he made,
sitting in perfect stillness, as
the fire tore from him the body
that could not change the world
without losing itself. One moment
of flame is the heart of patience.
Fire curls around the head, yes,
like a wreath, like tongues, like
paper birds too slender to fly. Why,
then, does the body curl into the pose
of a fighter if not from rage? Not ten
days, no, but five I sat with your body
as you, neither curled nor wreathed
in flame, lay in a hospital bed, floating
so far from me that if holding your
hand meant something, I couldn't
say what. I could say, as you lay
there, I would set myself on flame
to wake you, but I would not be able
to sit in such perfect stillness. Rage
the sinew, rage the supple flame
that curls like hands curl into claws
grasping the only body they will know.
Poor body that cannot realize images
will win in the end. Just turn another
page. The "scandal that has the whole
world buzzing" was not this living
cremation. Satellite photos were
improving our understanding of
pinwheeling typhoons in stretches
of ocean uncontaminated by land or
flame or the murder of NAACP field
workers. Allstate would insure your
life and your valuables. There were

bargains for acquisitions without
which no one would need cartridges
of film to record the intimacies of
the futile flesh. Take Carlo Bavagnoli's
superimposition of the dead Pope John
over a statue of Saint Veronica.
I can imagine how she hovered
in the wake of Christ, seeking
his blood, from the way she
hovers over the prone pontiff.
No sign of rage, no sign of love—
just the stony carapace of a body
beyond itself. In Beach Haven, NJ,
women watch a cable stretch under
the sea to send words to lands so
distant they seem not to exist. Perhaps
along these delicate cables traveled
news of the faraway: Harry Truman
immortalized in Greece, Lena Horne
dressed for a ball, not a funeral, Jacques
D'Amboise now Balanchine's Apollo,
raining golden arrows down upon
an indifferent earth, his body leaping
in stillness, holding its perfect form
so long it might seem he had passed
over to another life, his body never
curling in flame, never, in rage,
leaping away. If I assume you never
left me, not for one, not for five days,
will you allow me to hope Quang Duc
loved life more than he loved himself,
and that it was love he held in his
hands so tightly you would think,
looking at them, that they might break.

Blackout

November 9, 1965

I love you best in the dark: asleep
on the train, asleep on the stairs,
the city now stilled, the body itself

but now, somehow, no longer alone.
Asleep in the lobby, asleep in a chair,
I love you best in the dark, night's

curtain drawn. Come, night. Come
lovers in restaurants, in tunnels, in cars.
The body now still, the city at rest.

Asleep in the city, asleep at the wheel—
no one can see what you did in the light.
You're best in the dark. Night's curtain

descend and arise, oh moon, by fortune full:
reveal what hides, what's born, what dies.
The body won't flee, the city won't fight.

Love in the night, birth in the night, oh
hideous acts hiding in the light. Candles
and flares, I love you best in the dark.

Alone in the dark: together alone. What
is dark illumine, what is wretched hide.
Your body's a city recoiling from light.
Harmless in the dark, I think of you best.

The Pleasure of Being

November 12, 1965

The pleasure of being just what you are, John

        Lindsay, out of nowhere mayor-elect,

oh metropolis, the pleasure of being just where

        you are—center, stillpoint, unturning turnstile

of the world—oh crossroads! The pleasure of

        unimpeded motion, Ford Falcon, more than just

beauty the way the roads dusted up, it might

        as well have been the clouds passing by.

The pleasure of seeing in such fine, such rich detail

        the great and terrible things of the earth. The sweet,

the often bitter: oh most high flying bombers of Guam with

        your vicious payload leaving little of jungle

but cloud and dust and fire, oh hope of the finding of

        what may be left. The pleasure of the ambition not to

settle: Thurgood Marshall ascends, Solicitor General.

        Everyone was trying to be a genius in America.

America needed them so badly. The pleasure of reaching,

the pleasure of trying to touch, again, the hand of

God. The pleasure of remembering when once we did,

missiles poised, troops building, warships churning,

oh plan in the case of imminent distress.

Oh disaster averted—this time. Every time? The

pleasure of thinking so. The pleasure of those trained and

untamed bodies, the modern itself made flesh, how

they twist themselves into all the dreams

and terrors of the night: Merce Cunningham

a spotted leopard in repose, Martha Graham,

ruthless queen, martyring space. All

the heavens are burning. Oh pleasure of the burning,

the heavens being just what they are, burning just as

they are, whispering in the just night *hurry up, now,*

hurry up and taste.

Count

August 12, 1966

Count the ways: twelve make the body
stronger. Two sides divide the head:
between, a line of color. Three zebras
graze in rain near a watering hole near
the nicest hotel in Kenya. In 1966, $1,100
sent two people on safari. One star, Jack
Palance, makes fourteen cocktails on
one yacht with a single bottle of finest
liquor. Six simple steps ensure the body
wracked by infirmity will not fall when
crossing thresholds. The third step *(turn
the handle)* precedes the fourth *(open
the door)*. Five letters address the subject
of one previous issue in which one feature
featured "The Unlikeliest Poet." In '66 this
was James Dickey. Only one letter objected
to the title. Another objected to the dearth
of poets in America. Athens had 20,000
at its height. But none ever had to sing
of the ninety minutes, the twenty-nine floors,
the two hundred eighty feet, the twelve dead,
the thirty-one wounded, the one man, Charles
Whitman, no poet, barricaded in one tower.
Number of solitude, no number at all:
Count it anyway. Count two rings on the fingers of
Ramiro Martinez whose two hands covered
his face in the photo though he was the one
man who finally brought Whitman down from
his perch in the University of Texas clock tower.
Numberless were the motes in each puff
of smoke sent up (no language, this) from

the mouth of his rifle. Three: the number of
rifles. Two: the number of pistols. One:
the number of cans of peaches Whitman
carried up. Thirty: the number of the page
on which was captured a portrait of the killer
as a little boy: two his age, two rifles gripped
in two tiny hands, both guns standing taller
by mere inches than he was just at that
moment. One young boy on one red bicycle
on page fifty watches an honor guard of six
carry the solitary casket of Herm Wuertz, who
wrote an undetermined number of letters home
before dying two hours after noon on June 25,
1966, in an undisclosed location in Vietnam.
In photos of Massillon, Ohio (31,000 residents),
only one beauty queen waves in the sun while
hundreds of disposable hands point to what
would be sky were it not for the dark of
the factory that made gloves designed to fit
Asian hands. None of these hands touches
another. The mechanical forms are perfect
and undamaged. There are two families for
the war for every two against it. One man
says, "We have to beat them down" and
another one says, "Thou shalt not kill."
There is only one president in 1966 sending
four boys to war for every four who die.
That year: 6,143 deaths. By 1975: 58,217
deaths. Not all of them in coffins. Not all
of them in earth. Where was it that day—
the one variety of metal designed to keep
a .44 from bursting through to reach and kill
even the body strengthened twelve ways
to withstand uncontainable need blistering
from above, the clock in the photo frozen
at the very minute all things seemed to stand

perfectly still as if one as yet unheard voice
called every gaze to the sky. On the cover of
the magazine, the space where bullets ripped
eyeholes in glass. Count them. Tell me there's
a way to make up the numbers. Two eyes broken
open for each body: one flesh, one life caught
in crossfire rocketing through crystalline sky.

Sting Like a

1.

If an "athlete" is a
prizewinner but
a "hero" is a god,
which did you want
to be? What prize
on the shores of
history did you seek
with fist and rage and
whip-sharp tongue?

2.

Ovid on the Black Sea, like
Cassius Clay in Lewiston
to fight in the dark woods
of history. Only he wasn't
anymore, not "Cassius,"
not his namesake Cassius
Marcellus Clay, the lion
of White Hall, son of Green,
father of Sally. Greater still
his namesake so many years
later. What is crime to such
men? Like Ovid's, was
his not a crime of love?

3.

To be hit by blows you can't even see
is to know the lure, is to know the speed,
is to witness stars stoke fires in the sea.

With iron fists and a beautiful tan
a man is one who knows that *to be*
hit by blows you can't even see

is to suffer in rage, suffer no peace:
leaving is freedom, exile is here
watching stars fall to choke in the seas.

The iron fist is a broken pen he
wields with a speed that knows that grief
is *to be hit by blows you can't even see.*

Justice is the riddle of what should be
as cat plays mouse, as mosquito pulls plow,
as the tireless stars take swings at the sea.

A story is a man who learns that to be
is *to turn out the lights* and sing to the sea:
to be hit by blows you can't even see
is to sting like a sting like a sing like a bee.

4.

Cassius, unbending in
your righteous rage,
you put your fist
through 1968
though you would
not fight in any ring:

We don't take part
in Christian wars,
you said. You fought
the law and the law
won and then it didn't.
Is hatred the price of
speech? Untie your
gloves, gentle Cassius,
and lead us back to
the Black Seas you
watched crash against:
the white sands, those waves,
like you, *as big as all history.*

5.

Do you remember when
everything was burning?
Everything a lit wick,
everything a prelude to ash.
At that very time when
all the world was alive
with whip-sharp flame,
tradition reports the fires
left the hero an open path.

Broken Obelisk

April 12, 1968

Barnett Newman's *Broken Obelisk,* built broken in 1963, moved to Houston in 1969 and then broke for real in 2004.

Cleaned, righted, and broken now as intended, the obelisk was at last dedicated, thirty-five years after the city of Houston refused to make it a monument to the memory of Martin Luther King.

Martin Luther was a prince of the church that broke in two before breaking into ever smaller pieces.

In how many pieces did America break in 1968?

In 1968, it seemed Vietnam would be less battered as now bombing "would be sharply limited." Look, the great man, Lyndon Johnson, suffers the awesome weight and duties of office. In the picture he hunches broken over a page of broken words.

The great men of Egypt, so intriguing, preferred in death to sleep in comfort beneath the weight of tons of glistening sand, now at least unseen by the ever-watchful sun. If you knew in what darknesses to look, you'd see thirty centuries of greatness sealed in rock, silent, as they say, as the grave.

I don't know how they could print it—how could they not—the shot of Martin Luther King broken on the ground. You can see the blood pooling black on the balcony if you peer through the wrought iron cage of the railings. A single white handkerchief could not quite cover his face, his eyes closed as if sleeping, his fingers so slightly, so delicately curled, his leg bent at the knee as if he might still rise up.

Egyptian pharaohs knew they would rise as if from a gentle sleep. If they were well prepared, buried with slaves and riches to bribe the ferryman, they would live as kings again.

Tell me, kings of Memphis, how long did it take you to chase the killer through the streets adjacent to the Lorraine Hotel? You would not find him there, not in Memphis, not with his finger curled to touch the whole world all at once.

The shot is clear. Three men point to a sky without a sun.

Carved in earth, in the manner of prayer, one Egyptian priest wrote, "Beautiful are the things you have done on earth." I think, just then, he too was speaking about the sun.

There was only one tragedy this week, LIFE said. It is hopeful, LIFE said, that the bombs will slow and that Johnson will not run. The murder in Memphis was not in Egypt, LIFE said, though the tombs were so real, suddenly, in the pictures. Osiris, LIFE said, ruled over life and death. Why is it always the warrior-kings we hope will return? Some kings do not come back. The earth shudders under its own weight. The earth is quieter than it was eight days ago. The earth will spin on, LIFE said, and I wanted to believe.

I believe it was three days after King lay broken on that hotel balcony that Nina Simone called him the king of love. If she'd seen these pictures, she would have seen the face of a man with lips almost parted.

Broken Obelisk took its place by a chapel in which no one preaches. Rothko's walls, silent as dark tombs, have taken the anger to them. Is this, then, peace? On the benches, outside the chapel, books of every shape and color rest. The obelisk, too, rests. It hovers over a pool with water so thin you can't drink it. It will always be broken. It will not fall.

Look: it is as if the great man is about to speak.

Shot

October 29, 1971

Don't be distracted by
the shot of Picasso,
the flesh sagging
its frame. No cubist,
this body aged 90:
the hands lively
because they could
still be. On the facing
page, a woman as old
as Picasso watches
the Portugal sun slip
from her grasping hands,
shadows painting craggy
walkways to eternity.
Soon, it will all be gone.
She wears black because
she knows it will be so.
Youth flees at the first
sign of trouble, which
is its charm. But this
is not the real story.
The real story can't
begin at the end. Even
those wizened bodies
were once sweet, whole
if not wholesome, even
toothy, grinning like David
Cassidy holding his guitar
as everyone in 1971
wanted to be held. Oh
David, imagine little
could ever be wrong

in the world, and you
might dance at the Shah's
party, on the shores of
the Seychelles, with
anyone who never
felt as beautiful and
free as the foolish
tufts of your hair.
You were clear and
young and capable of
making a nation lose
its head. Should I be
sad, on a night like
this, that you were no
Picasso or that such
loves never last?
Tonight it is so calm
I see before me all
that was once elusive.
I know and understand
the way longing withers
a body. Every train
passes with the same
insistence—*to be young,*
to be young—,
which is to be so
desperate to be loved
what wouldn't you do
for the men who promise,
in the night, they will
carve your willing flesh
into the shape you know
you deserve to be.

Union

April 28, 1972

No paper to stain, no contract to bind.

The hand that grasps a bloody mist grasps nothing.

A bull flipping over and over its horns.

Favor me with your eye, favor me with your lip.

Drawn between them, the man and the woman.

For this I spent, for this I labored?

Coal in its obsolescence, steam in its ever-presence.

A hand grasps a hand grasping another hand.

What was it you said?

Oh, corporation, fast-breeding: new day, new world.

Every whisper and glance instant festivity.

If you look at the sea, you see churning flowers.

The sheet winds and winds and winds.

Whose hands about my heart, what knot tight in my throat?

Witness, you say, eager to be perceived.

One hand a flower, one a torch.

Made for the cleansing, made for the tethering.

One alone I asked to see me. Alone, one would.

What perfect, what union?

First Earth

December 29, 1972

First nothing, then a tear.
How the language would
not disambiguate the page:
tear, tear. You may have
just said them the same
way in your head, your
lips not moving, not like
Ambrose tracing the shape
of the heard with unruly
tongue. Heard, herd: all
the people came to watch,
like Augustine, fascinated
by the spectacle of a man
reading silently. What
was the man saying, alone,
to himself in the dark?
Lip of the world, edge of
the composition of what is
reasonable to include. Yet
what rose up outside of
the pages if not a single
jewel? Earth, in your
bending totality, curving
always away even from
the very frame of *life*
as it is. A tear hanging
in the sky or was it a tear
through which worlds
as yet unheralded might
appear? Imagine it all
different now: one Earth,

people in cafes speaking
of a gentle symbolism,
all words now directed to
the one face from which
we could no longer turn.
Oh fearless, oh righteous,
oh tiny, pendant world,
strung as if from the neck
of a jealous lover: I could
almost swear you'd let me
touch you all at once.

Looking into *The Book of LIFE*

Much traveled, yes, always in realms of yellowed
paper, black and white and blue: the whole
a globe in a book in a box and on each page
a face, a name, some wonders of use and want.
Was this how it began? A boy who stared
at stars, a boy in love with the moon. A swirl,
some sheer and stirring roundness that was sky.
Apollo, now that I have opened the book, it is
so quiet I can hear beneath the dense
and layered noise of life. So little of
my body that will last, and those I love
now fade to black before my eyes. You pass.
Far-darter, light-bringer, tell me what's true:
Living is not coming to be but passing away.

Notes

Walt Whitman called America the greatest poem ever written. And so one prominent task of American poets became calling into being the America they need or dream. What an opportunity and what a problem: deciding whose America it is and how it should be imagined or remembered. My America, what little piece I call (and yet is not) mine, was captured before my life began in the pages of LIFE magazine. These poems call back to life what was then already history. Dated poems in the first and third sections refer to issues of the magazine. All details present in the poems are present in corresponding issues, which is a founding premise and constraint of these poems. The exceptions are closely related to LIFE and are: "Imagine the Moon: September 12, 1962," "Sting Like a," and "First Earth: December 29, 1972." The middle section contains poems of the life that began in the wake of the end of LIFE as Americans knew it and, in some equally improbably way, the end of America as LIFE knew it. Endings are and are not elegy.

First Issue: December 23, 1936
Volume 1, number 1. Cover: Fort Peck Dam, Montana. Photographer: Margaret Bourke-White. Art Deco Construction of the Dam: Crenellations and Shadow. Franklin Roosevelt's Wild West. Chinatown School. Curry of Kansas. Brazil. Fort Knox. Fort Belvedere. Russia Relaxes. Private Lives. Black Widow. LIFE Goes to a Party. Price: 10 cents

Late in '38: October 17, 1938
Volume 5, number 16. Cover: Carole Lombard, close-up. Unsmiling. Curled silver-blonde hair. She stares out as if distracted. Photographer: Albert Eisenstadt. They called her "the Screwball Girl." Picture of the week: "London Newsboy Sells the Biggest News of the World." In the photo he holds in one hand a newspaper and in the other a sign reading "PEACE" in large block letters. Chamberlain Has His Triumph. War in China Gambles

for Asia's Future. Queen Elizabeth Christens the "Queen Elizabeth." Garbo Returns. Tweed Goes to the Night Clubs. Price: 10 cents.

Praise for the Snow: April 17, 1944

Volume 16, number 16. Cover: Hollywood's Prettiest. A starlet in a bathing costume leans against a large cutout shaped like a seashell. Spring Snow in Central Park. Dead Soldiers' Effects. Tarawa Revisited. Wisconsin Primary. America's World Purpose. Volcanoes: Paracutin and Vesuvius. British Rocket Gun. Bathing Beauty. Hedda Hopper's Hats. Tiger Cubs. LIFE Goes to a War Plant Beauty Dance. Price: 10 cents.

Meanwhile the World: February 9, 1948

Volume 24, number 6. Cover: Robert A. Taft: Republican Presidential Candidates. Photographer: Nina Leen. Young Man Stands on Head Before 48 State Capitols. India Loses Her 'Great Soul.' Stunt Skater Gets Singed. The U.S. Runs Short of Oil. A Day in Lincoln's Life. Ancient Mariners. Snow Fashions. How Hot Can a Man Get? Price: 15 cents.

Grip the Rope: March 6, 1950

Volume 28, number 10. Cover: Marsha Hunt in "The Devil's Disciple." Photographer: Philippe Halsman. Coal Strike Threatens a Crisis. Grocer Tests the Law with 39 Cent Wine. Boxer Dies from Blow in Ring. The Case for Distinguished Corpses. The White Queen. Lost Treasures of the Americas. Weird Amphibians. "Black Light" Art. Week of my father's birth. Price: 20 cents.

A Shirt Loves a Body: December 7, 1953

Volume 35, number 23. Cover: What Makes Audrey Charm. Audrey Hepburn in a man's white dress shirt. Sits in profile, head turned to stare out at the camera, holding a phone to her ear. Does she meet your gaze? Photographer: Mark Shaw. Racers Challenge Death in Mexico. After 22 Years "Dead" Couple Turns Up. The Day the First Man Flew. Good-For-Nothing Gifts. Trying Elephants For Size. Too Rugged for the Marines? Week of my mother's birth. Price: 20 cents.

Fall of a Star: April 20, 1959
Volume 46, number 16. Cover: A Comic Marilyn Sets Movie Aglow.
Photographer: Richard Avedon. Space Voyagers Are Rarin' to Go. How
the West Was Won, Part III. How and When to Plant Marigolds, Petunias,
Pansies. Maria Meneghini Callas Tells Her Own Story. Holy Images on
Dashboards. Tender Scene at Bad Creek, Ky., as Baby Is Born. Price: 25 cents.

Fall of a Star: November 9, 1959
Volume 47, number 19. Cover: Celebs Leap for Camera. Photographer:
Philippe Halsman. Sights You Have Never Seen. Baffling U.S. Art: What Is
It About? Why in the World Are the Windsors Jumping? De Gaulle's View
of Himself. Best Pancakes for All Meals. New Nobel Literary Row. New
Aerial Camera. The Shah's Happiest Return. No price on cover.

Imagine the Moon: September 12, 1962, refers not to an issue
of *LIFE* magazine but to a speech delivered by John F. Kennedy at Rice
University. The poem cites Buzz Aldrin, the second man on the moon,
arguably the first poet to visit the moon, who said, "Beautiful, beautiful.
Magnificent desolation."

A Face in the Mail: June 21, 1963
Volume 54, number 25. Cover: Shirley MacLaine as Irma la Douce.
Photographer: Gjon Mili. The Scandal That Has the Whole World Buzzing:
The Profumo Affair. The Empire-Shaking Scandal. A Buddhist Cremates
Himself. Assassin Kills a Negro Leader. Wild Young Summer Styles.
Vatican's Pageant of Sorrow. He-Man Ballet Dancer. Happy Family—
All at Sea. Miscellany: Pied Piper in the Pasture. Price: 25 cents.

Blackout: November 19, 1965
Volume 59, number 21. 5:28 p.m., November 9. Cover: The Lights Went
Out. In view looking east from Times Square during blackout, moon reflects
in windows of Union Carbide Building. Photographer: Henry Grossman.
Vive De Gaulle. A Dark Night to Remember. Trapped in a Skyscraper. Helen
Gurley Brown Turns Editor. Princess Margaret in America. Patterson's Glass
Jaw. The Kennedy Legacy. Cleveland's Stylishly Smashing Blondes. Let's Face
the Music. Price: 35 cents.

The Pleasure of Being: November 12, 1965

Volume 59, number 20. Cover: John Lindsay: Stunning Victory of a Loner. Photographer: Henri Dauman. A Prayer, a Take-off and The Strike: B-52s hit the Vietcong. Loner Lindsay's New York Triumph. Thurgood Marshall. Rhodesia. International Necklines. The Agony and the Ecstasy. The Year of Luxury Options. Untamed Surge of Modern Dance. Tiny Diva's Greatest Triumph. Great Dinners: Welsh Rabbit. Price: 35 cents.

Count: August 12, 1966

Volume 61, number 7. Cover: The Texas Sniper. Photographer: Shel Hershorn. Our Air and Water Can Be Made Clean. Waves of Summer Past and Present. Texas Sniper's Murderous Rampage. Sculptures in Motion. The Widening Credibility Gap. Murder—a Test of Our Times. Great Dinners. Price: 35 cents.

Sting Like a

This poem draws from several issues, including these: **November 30, 1962**, discusses Clay's "historical namesake" Cassius Marcellus Clay. **February 15, 1963**, features a poem by Cassius Clay with "I'm the Greatest" language from which I adapt in section three. **March 6, 1964**, covers Clay's defeat of Sonny Liston. **March 4, 1966**, discusses Clay's opposition to the Vietnam war. **October 25, 1968**, features Clay's response to the premiere of Howard Sackler's play *The Great White Hope* about boxing champion Jack Johnson, starring James Earl Jones.

Broken Obelisk: April 12, 1968

Volume 64, number 15. Cover: Week of Shock: Martin Luter King, 1929–1968. A later printing. The first runs did not yet have Joseph Louw's images of the dead Martin Luther King Jr., nor does the digitized issue on Google Books. Johnson's Bold Decision. Kings and Gods of Egypt. Wicked Go The Doors. The Death of Yuri Gagarin. The Death of Martin Luther King Jr. Also Consigned to Flame. Price: 35 cents.

Shot: October 29, 1971

Volume 71, number 18. Cover: David Cassidy: Teenland's Heartthrob. Photographer: Bob Peterson. Kings, Queens, and Emperors at the Shah's

Party. Running Back into the Past. Violent Harvest for Black Militants. Picasso at 90. The Continuing Trial of Jesse Hill Ford. Eye on the Environment. Parting Shots. Pierre Boulez Assessed. Week of my sister's birth. Price: 50 cents.

Union: April 28, 1972

Volume 72, number 16. Cover: The Marriage Experiments. Photographer: Ron D'Asaro. Living by Contract. Marriage in Trouble. Unmarried Parents. Frontier Partnerships. Collective Marriage. What's Happening to Marriage? Report from the Inferno: the Fighting in Vietnam Rages On. Price: 50 cents.

First Earth: December 29, 1972

Volume 73, number 25. Cover: LIFE's Last Issue: The Year in Pictures. The Waste of War. Footprint on the Moon. Nixon in China. Blood in Northern Ireland. Hostages in Munich. A Defiant Solzhenitsyn. Amin's Uganda. Phan Thi Kim Phuc Napalmed at the Tender age of 9. Mark Spitz's 7 Golds. Hurricane Agnes. Whatever Became of: Cassie Kernan, Judith Jamison, Bobby Lee Hunter, Bernice Gera, the Ivory-billed Woodpecker, Barbara Cochran, and David Phillip. None of this appears in the poem. The iconic "blue marble" image of the Earth, taken during Apollo 17 was not included in the final weekly issue of LIFE. Price: 50 cents.

Acknowledgments

I'm indebted to every library I've ever had the pleasure to visit, most especially the Johnstown Public Library in Johnstown, NY, where my mother worked for decades. That library gave a habitation and name to my early love of the written word and was the source of the initial *LIFE* magazines that sparked this project. Many thanks to the early readers of these poems, including Janet McAdams, Paul Otremba, and Amber Dermont. Many thanks to the eagle-eyed Becky Byron. Most especially, grateful thanks to Martha Collins who read it in every shape it took on its long, strange journey from a box of magazines buried in my closet to the words that appear on these very pages.

Poems from this collection have appeared in:

Kenyon Review, Michigan Quarterly Review, Plume, Poetry, Prairie Schooner, and *TriQuarterly.*

Every book I write is always also for my husband, Theodore Bale, whose life I cherish.